Presented to:

· ·

From:

· ·

Date:

· ·

The God of
Comfort

100 Bible Verses
to Soothe
Your Spirit

1

"Come to Me, all you
who labor and are
heavy laden, and I will
give you rest. Take My
yoke upon you and
learn from Me, for I
am gentle and lowly in
heart, and you will find
rest for your souls. For
My yoke is easy and
My burden is light."

MATTHEW 11:28–30

*I*n Jesus' day, Jewish people grew weary under the heavy load of expectations imposed on them by the Pharisees. In today's culture, we struggle with overbooked schedules, problems that threaten our peace, and the stress of everyday living. Jesus warned that we would have troubles (John 16:33), but He invites us to a different way of living. In an agricultural society, everyone understood a yoke went across the necks of two farm animals and connected them to the plow they were to pull.[1] A yoke didn't eliminate the burden, but it made the weight limit appropriate for the animals' abilities. In the same way, all Christ-followers will carry burdens, but we aren't called to take a load that is too heavy for us. Jesus invites us to trust Him with our troubles, and He promises rest for our souls when we do.

> *Father, help me to be faithful to fulfill the tasks You have given me. Please give me the strength to do my part. I will trust You to do what I cannot.*

2

If I say, "My foot slips,"
Your mercy, O Lord,
will hold me up.
In the multitude of my
anxieties within me,
Your comforts
delight my soul.

PSALM 94:18–19

*T*he Scriptures make it clear that many biblical writers struggled with fear and anxiety. In the Psalms, we read about a variety of human emotions, and anxiety was a frequent offender. It's notable that the writers of Scripture did not attempt to hide their anxiety. Instead, they cried out to God. In Psalm 94, the psalmist recalls how God dealt faithfully with him during a time of intense suffering (v. 18). Remembering God's faithfulness stirred his trust that God would be faithful to help in the future. Anxiety is a cruel tormentor, but it has the potential to drive us into a deeper relationship with God. It's one thing to read about God's love and consolation, and entirely another to experience it in a time of need. Undoubtedly, anxiety is a burden, but the psalmist was able to say of his history with God, "Your comforts delight my soul" (v. 19).

Father, I pray You will equip me to trust more and worry less. Calm my fears and increase my faith because You fulfill Your promises.

5

3

Anxiety in the heart of
man causes depression,
But a good word
makes it glad.

PROVERBS 12:25

$\mathcal{S}$ tress can cause a variety of medical issues, but nothing feels quite as hopeless as a heavy heart. Scripture teaches that a kind word is an antidote for a heart that has been weighed down by anxiety. A well-timed word has the potential to lift our spirits and motivate us to keep moving forward when we are tempted to quit. While it's true we can't control what other people say, we can be intentional about surrounding ourselves with encouraging people who aren't prone to speak negatively. When negative people surround us, we tend to expect the worst. On the other hand, it's beneficial to spend time with positive people because they tend to see the good in every situation and anticipate positive outcomes. A kind word can have a profound impact. We'd be wise to surround ourselves with people who speak kindly and to extend words of kindness every chance we get.

Lord, it is a blessing when You put people in my path who encourage me. Lead me to be quick to offer words of kindness and affirmation to those around me.

4

"Blessed is the man who
trusts in the Lord,
And whose hope is the Lord.
For he shall be like a tree
planted by the waters,
Which spreads out its
roots by the river,
And will not fear
when heat comes;
But its leaf will be green,
And will not be anxious
in the year of drought,
Nor will cease from
yielding fruit."

JEREMIAH 17:7–8

*T*he longer we walk with God, the more aware we become of our limitations. That awareness is not intended to discourage us; instead, it should motivate us to shift our confidence to God, who has no limitations. The prophet Jeremiah taught that those who trust in the Lord and place their confidence in Him will be blessed. He compares those who trust God to a tree with deep roots that is planted by a stream of water. Even during seasons of drought, when the conditions are unfavorable, those who trust continue to be productive because they rely on God's provision rather than their own limited resources. When we trust God, rather than ourselves, we have no reason to fear our weaknesses because they are no longer relevant. The Bible teaches that God's people are to trust Him for their every need. Regardless of what we lack, we can live with confidence because the God we serve lacks nothing.

> *Lord, I long to live productively, but Your Word reminds me I can do nothing apart from You. Teach me to abide in You so I can bear fruit for Your kingdom.*

5

"You cannot add any time
to your life by worrying
about it. If you cannot do
even the little things, then
why worry about the big
things? Consider how the
lilies grow; they don't work or
make clothes for themselves.
But I tell you that even
Solomon with his riches was
not dressed as beautifully
as one of these flowers."

LUKE 12:25–27 NCV

*W*orry is an indicator that we are focusing on a problem that is out of our control. When Jesus spoke to His disciples, He pointed out how unproductive it is to worry. No amount of worrying can add even one hour to our lives, but it has the potential to be destructive to our physical and mental well-being. Worry will do no good, but it can do much harm. To confront worry, Jesus instructed His disciples to contemplate the ways God is faithful to provide for all His creation. Wildflowers are on earth for just a short time and are much less valuable than human beings, but God provides for every flower in the field. Children of God do not need to waste time and energy worrying about things God has already promised. When we are tempted to worry, we can always redirect our thoughts to God's promises.

Father, You are faithful to provide for Your people. Help me to be mindful of all the ways You have provided for me, and increase my confidence that You will provide in the future.

6

Don't worry about
anything; instead, pray
about everything. Tell
God what you need,
and thank him for all he
has done. Then you will
experience God's peace,
which exceeds anything
we can understand. His
peace will guard your
hearts and minds as
you live in Christ Jesus.

PHILIPPIANS 4:6–7 NLT

I n the book of Philippians, the apostle Paul provided his readers with a prescription for anxiety. When confronted with a problem that makes us anxious, Paul said the first thing we should do is pray. The natural response to troubling circumstances is to worry, but that's not how Paul instructed us to respond. Paul taught that if we take our problem to God in prayer, petitioning Him for what we need and thanking Him for the ways He has already blessed us, God's peace will transcend our circumstances. Notice how Paul didn't encourage his audience to talk incessantly about the problem to family and friends; nor did he tell us to try to figure out the problem on our own. Instead, he prescribed prayer as the remedy. God does not intend for His people to use prayer as a last resort but, instead, as the first line of defense.

Father, I ask You to deepen my prayer life. When I am faced with trouble or tempted to worry, may my first inclination be to come to You. Teach me to devote myself to prayer.

7

When my father and my
mother forsake me,
Then the Lord will
take care of me.

PSALM 27:10

*A*t some point we will all be disappointed by someone we thought we could count on. Because of our sinful nature, all human beings are flawed; therefore, if we stay in any relationship long enough, we will be both disappointed and disappointing. As children we are taught to rely on our parents, but sometimes parents fail us. Even parents with the best intentions make mistakes. Sadly, some parents inflict serious harm on their children. It's painful when someone we trust betrays us, but we can be confident that God never will. Healthy relationships are a blessing, and we should be thankful for the good people in our lives. But we must be mindful that God is the only One who is capable of having our best interest in mind at all times. The Scriptures promise that God will never leave or forsake us (Hebrews 13:5), and He is always committed to our good (Romans 8:32).

> *Father, I pray my relationships will be well-balanced and healthy. Thank You for the people in my life, but help me to remember I have needs that only You can meet.*

8

Trust in the L{ORD} with
all your heart,
And lean not on your
own understanding;
In all your ways
acknowledge Him,
And He shall direct
your paths.

PROVERBS 3:5–6

*P*roverbs is known as the book of wisdom. Naturally we all want to make wise decisions, but there are times in life when it's difficult to know how to proceed. When we encounter a season when we can't see a clear path forward, we often attempt to figure things out on our own. Usually this leads to a dead-end road of frustration. King Solomon, the author of much of the book of Proverbs, offers a solution. He instructs us not to try to figure things out on our own but to trust God with a whole heart and obey Him in every area of our lives. God's ways are often beyond our understanding (Isaiah 55:8–9). However, He invites us into a relationship where we know Him so intimately that even when we don't understand what the next step is, we trust that He will lead us on the right path.

Father, even when I don't understand what is happening, I will have confidence in Your goodness. Help me to trust that every outcome will be for my ultimate good and Your glory.

9

I am convinced that
neither death nor life,
neither angels nor
demons, neither the
present nor the future,
nor any powers, neither
height nor depth, nor
anything else in all
creation, will be able to
separate us from the
love of God that is in
Jesus Christ our Lord.

ROMANS 8:38–39 NIV

*W*e all fear the loss of people and things we care about. It causes a tremendous amount of stress in all human beings. We fear losing our health, loved ones, jobs and financial security, and a host of other things that bring us joy and comfort. And to be sure, sometimes we lose things we rely on and love deeply. At some point we all experience loss. But above all things, Christians depend on the love of Christ. Jesus' love is our primary need, and without it we would be doomed. Thankfully, the Scriptures teach that Christ's love cannot be lost. The apostle Paul makes it clear that there is no disaster or calamity, no sin or circumstance that can separate us from the love of Christ. Christ's love is the thing we need most. It cannot be taken from us, and we can rely on it all our days.

Father, Your Word says without love I have nothing. Help me to be constantly aware of Christ's love for me and to live in a way that demonstrates His love to others.

10

"Peace I leave with
you; my peace I give to
you. Not as the world
gives do I give to you.
Let not your hearts
be troubled, neither
let them be afraid."

JOHN 14:27 ESV

*J*esus longs for His followers to live in His peace. Just before going to the cross, Jesus described the invitation of peace to His disciples. The peace Jesus offers is only found by being in a right relationship with God. Sometimes we wrongly assume living in peace means living a life free of conflict, but that's an incorrect assessment. The peace of Christ does not depend on outward circumstances, but rather on Christ's atoning work on the cross, which puts us in right relationship with the Father. The world attempts to counterfeit the peace Christ offers, but Jesus' peace cannot be duplicated. Apart from Jesus, there is no genuine peace, but for Christ-followers, peace is ours for the taking. When we know our relationship with God is right because of Christ's sacrifice on the cross, our hearts can be at peace and our fears can be silenced.

Father, thank You for the peace I have in You. Regardless of the situation, I will cling to You in all circumstances. Empower me to live in Your peace every day.

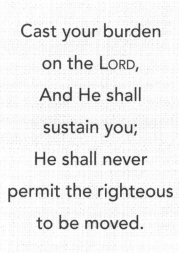

11

Cast your burden
on the LORD,
And He shall
sustain you;
He shall never
permit the righteous
to be moved.

PSALM 55:22

*K*ing David had legitimate reasons to worry. As king of Israel, he dealt with political enemies who wanted him dead, the day-to-day responsibilities of being the nation's ruler, devastating family problems, and personal sin that nearly destroyed him. But David understood that God doesn't intend for His children to carry the burden of anxiety about their own sin. When David sinned with Bathsheba, he confessed and repented (Psalm 51). During times of stress, he cried out to God (55:1–2). David was a man who communicated with God. It's notable that David instructed his readers, "Cast your burden on the LORD." When we are struggling with a circumstance that is threatening our peace, it's tempting to try to fix the problem ourselves. But God doesn't expect us to figure things out and muster up strength on our own. The Bible instructs us to take our problems to God in prayer and trust that He will give us the help we need.

Father, I am surrounded by worrisome things that are out of my control. But Lord, You are in total control. I place those things at Your feet and pray You will intervene.

12

So we may boldly say:

"The LORD is my helper;

I will not fear.

What can man

do to me?"

HEBREWS 13:6

*T*o some degree, most of us want to be well thought of by others. But seeking approval can be costly. When we are preoccupied with what other people think of us, we unwittingly shift our focus away from God. Of course, Christians are called to love other people (Mark 12:31). But the Bible warns about seeking the approval of others. Paul wrote, "Am I now trying to win the approval of human beings, or of God? Or am I trying to please people? If I were still trying to please people, I would not be a servant of Christ" (Galatians 1:10 NIV). Christ-followers are called to live for God's approval (2 Timothy 2:15). When we are mindful that the Lord is our constant source of help, we can rest in the fact that regardless of what other people say or do, we have no reason to fear.

Father, please help me to be kind and loving to all people but to live my life for an audience of One. I am committed to pleasing You.

13

Why are you cast
down, O my soul?
And why are you
disquieted within me?
Hope in God, for I
shall yet praise Him
For the help of His
countenance.

PSALM 42:5

The Psalms provide plenty of evidence to suggest that King David cultivated the excellent habit of speaking to himself rather than listening to whatever thought came to his mind. When we are feeling depressed or anxious, we are often overcome with negative thinking. Foolishly, we replay negative thoughts and what-ifs over and over in our minds. The Scriptures teach us a better way. In Psalm 42, we see that David was experiencing a season of depression. Instead of entertaining the negative thoughts that inevitably came to his mind, David interrupted those thoughts with his own dialogue. David coached himself to put his hope in God, and he resolved to be a man who praised God. We have the ability to accept or reject every thought that comes to mind. We can refuse to entertain negative thoughts and replace them with the truths of God's Word.

Father, teach me to encourage myself with truths about Your character. Please empower me to cultivate an excellent thought life that is based on truth.

14

We are hard pressed
on every side, but not
crushed; perplexed,
but not in despair;
persecuted, but
not abandoned;
struck down, but
not destroyed.

2 CORINTHIANS 4:8–9 NIV

*C*hristians are not immune to hardship. In fact, Jesus warned that as long as we are in this world, we will have troubles (John 16:33). But as Christ-followers face problems, we have the privilege of relying on God's power rather than our own. When Paul wrote to the church at Corinth, he didn't sugarcoat the difficulties he was facing. He admitted that he and his colleagues were "hard pressed on every side, but not crushed" and "perplexed, but not in despair." A casual reader of Scripture might wonder how that could be the case. How could Paul and his colaborers endure such affliction without being destroyed? Paul said, "We have this treasure in jars of clay to show that this all-surpassing power is from God and not from us" (2 Corinthians 4:7 NIV). Paul knew he had to rely on God's power rather than his own. Our resources, as human beings, are limited, but God's power is infinite.

> *Father, there is nothing that is too difficult for You. My resources are limited, but Your power is infinite. Please act on my behalf and do what only You can do.*

15

The LORD is my

shepherd;

I shall not want.

He makes me to lie

down in green pastures;

He leads me beside

the still waters.

He restores my soul.

PSALM 23:1–3

$\mathcal{T}$ he metaphor of the Lord as our Shepherd in Psalm 23 is a powerful one. Sheep are vulnerable animals who tend to lose their way and need constant care. Eastern shepherds were responsible for protecting their sheep, providing for their needs, and leading them in the right direction. But not all shepherds were good ones, and some shepherds didn't care for their flocks. In John 10, Jesus described Himself this way: "I am the good shepherd. The good shepherd gives His life for the sheep" (v. 11). Jesus provides for our needs, He gives us rest, and He revives our souls. As members of Christ's flock, we must walk close to our Shepherd. As we receive His loving care, we find refreshment for our souls.

Jesus, You are the Good Shepherd, and You provide refreshment for my soul. Thank You for Your compassion and kindness. Help me to follow closely and never wander from Your flock.

16

"[God] will wipe away
every tear from their
eyes, and there will
be no more death,
sadness, crying, or
pain, because all the
old ways are gone."

REVELATION 21:4 NCV

D uring times of grief, depression, or loss, it's tempting to believe seasons of sadness will never come to an end. It's easy to buy into the lies that things will never change or that problematic situations will never improve. But the Bible teaches that a time is coming on God's kingdom calendar when we will shed our last tear. A day is coming when there will no longer be any death, sorrow, tears, or pain. As Christians, we can rely on God's promise that our seasons of suffering will not last forever. Our best days are always ahead of us. The apostle Paul experienced more suffering than most, and as a result he kept his eyes fixed on the promise of eternity. He wrote, "'What no eye has seen, what no ear has heard, and what no human mind has conceived'— the things God has prepared for those who love him" (1 Corinthians 2:9 NIV).

Father, I know that every season of suffering will come to an end. Help me to focus on the fact that I will spend eternity with You, and my tears and hardships will be no more.

17

"Fear not, for I
am with you;
Be not dismayed,
for I am your God.
I will strengthen you,
Yes, I will help you,
I will uphold you
with My righteous
right hand."

ISAIAH 41:10

The most repeated phrase in the Bible is, "Do not fear." God knew His people would struggle with anxiety, and He repeatedly addressed the topic in the Scriptures. In Isaiah 41:10, God instructed His people not to fear because He was their God. Usually, when fear overwhelms us, it's because we are consumed by a situation that is beyond our control, and we are afraid of what might happen. But God instructs us to be mindful of His presence. The Bible promises that God will never leave us or forsake us (Hebrews 13:5), and therefore, we never face a problem alone. When we are aware of God's presence in every situation, we can shift our focus from our problem to God, who promises, "I will strengthen you, yes, I will help you" (Isaiah 41:10). God's provision arrives at the exact time we need it. The situation causing us anxiety may be out of our control, but nothing is beyond God's control.

Father, I do not want my life to be characterized by fear. Teach me to be continually aware of Your presence and live with confidence because You are always with me.

18

The Spirit God gave us
does not make us timid,
but gives us power, love
and self-discipline.

2 TIMOTHY 1:7 NIV

*G*od has not left us on our own to confront life's struggles. The Bible teaches that the Holy Spirit resides in every follower of Jesus Christ (John 14:17). The Holy Spirit fills many roles in the life of the believer, but sometimes we aren't mindful of His presence. When the apostle Paul wrote to Timothy, his spiritual son and protégé, Paul knew his own time on earth would soon come to an end (2 Timothy 4:6). The book of 2 Timothy is, in a sense, Paul's last will and testament. Paul knew Timothy struggled with fear, and Paul was writing to encourage him and to provide instruction on how to live as a faithful servant of Christ. Paul reminded Timothy that the Holy Spirit aids the believer in battling fear. As we learn to rely on the Holy Spirit, our fears subside, and we experience power, love, and increased degrees of self-discipline.

Lord, as I rely on the presence of the Holy Spirit within me, increase my power, love, and self-discipline so I can fulfill my calling and live a life that brings You glory.

19

"This is my command—
be strong and
courageous! Do not be
afraid or discouraged.
For the LORD your
God is with you
wherever you go."

JOSHUA 1:9 NLT

*A*fter Moses' death, Joshua was called by God to lead the Israelites into the promised land (Joshua 1:1–2). To put it mildly, it was a daunting task. God told Joshua three times to be strong and courageous (vv. 6–9). But what would be the source of Joshua's strength and courage? In verse 8, God instructed Joshua to speak of God's Word, meditate on the Word, and to obey God's Word. When we marinate our minds in the truths of Scripture, we are reminded of God's faithfulness, limitless power, and steadfast love. Our faith grows, and our fears shrink. God doesn't expect us to rely on our own resources. Left to ourselves, we don't have any reason to be confident. But when we rely on God's infinite power and flawless character, we have every reason to be the most courageous people in the world.

Father, teach me to think habitually about Your Word. Help my thoughts to be so steeped in Your promises that I can face any challenge with faith that You will do as You have said.

20

"Do not seek what you
are to eat and what
you are to drink, nor
be worried. For all the
nations of the world
seek after these things,
and your Father knows
that you need them."

LUKE 12:29–30 ESV

*M*any of us who live in the Western world spend an enormous amount of time thinking about material possessions. In a prosperous culture, excessive consumerism is a constant temptation. In other parts of the world, on the other hand, many people are forced to live day after day wondering whether they will have enough to cover the basic necessities. Jesus warned against being consumed with worry over our wants and even our needs. Jesus' words don't mean we shouldn't work hard and support ourselves (1 Thessalonians 4:11–12). The Bible teaches that Christians should be the hardest-working people in the workplace (Colossians 3:23–24). But the Christian life entails more than food and possessions. God calls us to a lifestyle of trusting Him for our needs. He has resources we don't possess and ways of providing that we are unaware of. Our heavenly Father knows what His children need, and He is faithful to provide (Genesis 22:14).

Father, I don't want to be entrapped by materialism. Help me to enjoy the things You have given me but never to exalt my possessions over my love and devotion for You.

21

Search me, O God,
and know my heart;
Try me, and know
my anxieties;
And see if there is any
wicked way in me,
And lead me in the
way everlasting.

PSALM 139:23–24

*P*rayer is one of the most effective spiritual disciplines when it comes to dealing with anxiety. King David enjoyed a vibrant prayer life, and Psalm 139 is evidence that David prayed with transparency. David asked God to take inventory of his heart and mind and to remove the things that were offensive. As Christ-followers we don't want to harbor anything in our hearts, minds, or habits that is offensive to the Lord or harmful to our faith. Our thought life has the potential to make us either anxious or peaceful. David wisely petitioned God to reveal to him errors in his thought pattern that didn't align with God's truth. God knows the source of our stress and anxiety far better than we do, and He has the ability to instruct us in a better way to think and live. We can rely on His leadership into the way everlasting.

> *Lord, I don't want a single thing to remain in me that is offensive to You. Please remove everything that does not align with Your will for my life.*

22

Where God's love is,
there is no fear, because
God's perfect love
drives out fear. It is
punishment that makes
a person fear, so love
is not made perfect in
the person who fears.

1 JOHN 4:18 NCV

*T*he Bible often speaks of the "fear of the Lord." This refers to a believer's reverence, respect, and awe of God, rather than the emotion of feeling afraid. But the apostle John wrote about the negative emotion of fear in today's verse. Before we get to know God well, we might be prone to worry about how He will respond to our problems. What if He allows us to suffer for a season? What if He doesn't intervene as quickly as we'd like? As we grow closer to God and understand His faithfulness and goodness, we trust Him more. We gain clarity about His love for us, and we realize that everything God permits in our lives is ultimately for our good (Romans 8:28). The more we understand God's love for us, and the more we grow in our love for God, the less fear we will experience.

Father, I want to grow in my knowledge of You. Increase my understanding of Your character, ways, and attributes, and permit me the privilege of knowing You well.

23

Say to those who are
fearful-hearted,
"Be strong, do not fear!
Behold, your God will
come with vengeance,
With the recompense
of God;
He will come and
save you."

ISAIAH 35:4

*A*n encouraging word during a time of stress can be like water to a parched throat. The prophet Isaiah instructed his readers to be strong and not to fear. Isaiah offered hope with these words: "Your God will come." When we are waiting on a situation to change, we might begin to wonder if God will ever intervene. But Isaiah's words remind us that God is faithful. At times we will be forced to wait longer than we would like, but during those times God strengthens our faith and deepens our trust. God never promised us that life would be comfortable, so we shouldn't be surprised by trouble when it comes. But as we wait for God to act, we have the potential to grow closer to Him, to know Him better, and to love Him more. As our history develops with God, our faith grows, and we become strong in the Lord.

> *Lord, teach me to wait on You. Help me to resist the urge to act on my own and get ahead of Your timing. As I wait, I will draw closer to You.*

24

The LORD will fight
for you; you need
only to be still.

EXODUS 14:14 NIV

When the people of Israel were fleeing from Egypt and Pharaoh's evil regime, they had reason to be afraid. Pharaoh was a man of authority, and the Egyptians had oppressed the Israelites. Without God's help, the Israelites were no match for Pharaoh and his armies. As the Egyptians gained ground, the Israelites feared for their lives. They wondered aloud to Moses if they were going to die (Exodus 14:11). Moses told them, "The LORD will fight for you; you need only to be still." Moses' words proved true when the Lord parted the Red Sea so the Israelites could pass by on dry ground (v. 22). And so it is with us. When we are threatened by overwhelming opposition, the answer isn't a better battle strategy or increased effort. We are called to trust God. He faithfully fights for His children and provides in ways we never could on our own.

Father, I am prone to the sin of self-reliance, and I ask You to forgive me. Teach me to rely exclusively on You. I acknowledge that You alone are my hope and my strength.

25

The LORD is my light
and my salvation;
Whom shall I fear?
The LORD is the
strength of my life;
Of whom shall
I be afraid?

PSALM 27:1

*D*avid likely wrote Psalm 27 before he was king and during the time he was exiled from his home and being hunted by King Saul and his men.[2] David was being followed by a group of enemies who wanted to kill him (v. 2). Despite David's terrifying situation, he remained confident in the Lord. David had cultivated the habit of encouraging himself with truths about God. He said, "The Lord is the strength of my life; of whom shall I be afraid?" When we are confronted with situations that cause anxiety, we do well to encourage ourselves with the promises of Scripture. David didn't focus on the men who were trying to kill him. Instead, he spent his time thinking about the power and goodness of God. As a result, even in the midst of great stress, David could say, "Of whom shall I be afraid?" (v. 1).

> *Father, there are plenty of reasons to be fearful and anxious. Teach me to be confident in Your provision regardless of the situation. Lord, please increase my faith.*

26

I pray that the God
who gives hope will
fill you with much
joy and peace while
you trust in him.
Then your hope will
overflow by the power
of the Holy Spirit.

ROMANS 15:13 NCV

*I*n modern culture, the concept of hope is passive. For instance, we "hope" it doesn't rain on Saturday. Biblical hope, however, is not passive but is characterized by anticipation. Biblical hope is defined as "trustful expectation, particularly with reference to the fulfillment of God's promises."[3] As Christians, we serve the "God who gives hope" and are called to be people of hope. As we face difficult circumstances, we have the privilege of clinging to the promises of God and believing God will bring His promises to pass in our circumstances. As we wait, we are wise to remind ourselves of God's promises. As we do, we experience the joy and peace that accompanies trust. Christians are not called to live lives of defeat. As people of hope, we wait with anticipation that God will do as He said.

Father, I am filled with anticipation. Teach me to abound in hope and to look forward to seeing Your promises fulfilled both in this life and the life to come.

27

God is our refuge
and strength,
an ever-present
help in trouble.
Therefore we will
not fear, though the
earth give way
and the mountains fall
into the heart of the sea.

PSALM 46:1–2 NIV

*I*t's likely that King Hezekiah wrote Psalm 46 after God delivered Jerusalem from the Assyrians (2 Kings 18–19).[4] Undoubtedly, in the midst of political upheaval and the threat of destruction, the people of Zion felt as if their world were falling apart. But even during times of turmoil, God's people have reason to be confident. Hezekiah described God as "our refuge and strength" and "an ever-present help in trouble" (Psalm 46:1 NIV). God has the ability to protect His people in any circumstance, and His power is unlimited. God is not deterred by threats of war, natural disasters, violence, terrorism, or any catastrophe. Regardless of the situation, there is no need for us to fear, because God does not abandon His people in times of trouble.

Father, I pray You will surround me with a hedge of protection. Keep me safe in times of trouble. Help me to remember You are in control and that You love me.

28

Do not be afraid of
sudden terror,
Nor of trouble from the
wicked when it comes.

PROVERBS 3:25

*D*uring stressful times it's easy to live with a sense of impending doom. Although we can't put our finger on what's wrong, we live with a chronic uneasiness, afraid the bottom is about to fall out. We might imagine worst-case scenarios and make ourselves increasingly anxious by continually asking, "What if?" The writer of today's verse warned about such thinking. While it's true that we can't control the future, many of the catastrophes we worry about never happen. When we walk in God's will for our lives and apply God's wisdom to our daily living, we will avoid many of the disasters that befall the wicked. Regardless of what comes our way, we can trust that God will strengthen us with His grace the moment we need it. Until then, there is no point in worrying about things that may never happen.

Father, teach me to manage my thoughts and to avoid worrying about what might happen. Help me to be more influenced by my faith than by fear.

29

"Do not be anxious about your life, what you will eat or what you will drink, nor about your body, what you will put on. Is not life more than food, and the body more than clothing?"

MATTHEW 6:25 ESV

$\mathcal{T}$he Bible calls us to be good stewards of our resources and to be wise with money. Still, there is no such thing as "financial security." If we aren't careful, material wealth gives us a false impression of security that has the potential to damage our faith. Jesus instructed His followers not to worry about basic needs of food and clothing because God is faithful to provide for His people. Jesus warned there is more to life than materialism. The more resources we acquire, the more tempting it is to place our trust in our material wealth rather than trusting God to provide for us. The Scriptures teach that if our riches increase, we shouldn't set our hearts on them (Psalm 62:10). Our hearts belong to Jesus, not to our personal resources.

Lord, teach me to have a healthy view about money and material possessions. I want to manage my resources well without placing too much emphasis on them.

30

Because you have made the
LORD, who is my refuge,
Even the Most High,
your dwelling place,
No evil shall befall you,
Nor shall any plague come
near your dwelling;
For He shall give His
angels charge over you,
To keep you in all your ways.

PSALM 91:9–11

*T*he author of Psalm 91 wrote about the risks of living in an unsafe world. At the time the psalm was written, health care was primitive at best. Deadly plagues, pestilence, traps, and wildlife were common threats. Today we face different challenges. In modern-day society we deal with terrorism, gun violence, road rage, drug overdoses, and a long list of other maladies. Although the nature of the threats has changed, the source of believers' protection has not. Of course, the Bible and our personal experiences have taught us that Christians are not immune to hardship or catastrophes. But God protects His people from countless disasters. As children of God, we can rest in the confidence that everything that happens to us is filtered by the Father, and nothing can befall us that He doesn't work for our own good (Matthew 10:30; Romans 8:28).

> *Father, I'm grateful nothing catches You off guard. Protect me from disaster, and keep me safe in an unsafe world. Teach me to rely solely on You.*

31

"God clothes the grass
in the field, which
is alive today but
tomorrow is thrown
into the fire. So how
much more will God
clothe you? Don't
have so little faith!"

LUKE 12:28 NCV

*G*od provides for all of His creation. King David wrote, "You open Your hand and satisfy the desire of every living thing" (Psalm 145:16). Unlike animals and plant life, human beings bear the image of God (Genesis 1:26–27). Jesus made this point to His disciples by arguing from the greater to the lesser. Jesus said that if God cared for the grass of the field, which is here for a short time, then He would surely care for people, who are made in His image. Jesus communicated to His disciples that their worry signaled a lack of faith. Worry is deceptive, and it blinds us to the ways God provides for His creation.[5] Of course, Jesus wasn't suggesting we live lazy lives, waiting for God to provide for us. Even animals have to work to secure their food. Jesus asks us to trust God and use the abilities and opportunities He entrusts to us.

> *Father, thank You for all the ways You provide for me. I will not worry about being in need, but rather I will have faith that trusts in Your provision.*

32

I sought the LORD,

and He heard me,

And delivered me

from all my fears.

PSALM 34:4

*A*nxiety can be a blessing if it drives us to Jesus. Psalm 34 makes it clear that King David was experiencing fear. David didn't pretend that everything was fine, nor did he attempt to address his fears on his own. David said, "I sought the LORD." Fear can be so crippling it can bring us to the end of ourselves. Although it doesn't seem like it, coming to the end of ourselves is a good thing. Self-reliance is a sin that keeps us from experiencing a vibrant relationship with Jesus. In the midst of David's fear, he sought the Lord, and David wrote, "[He] delivered me from all my fears." Once we realize that self-reliance is a fallacy, we can experience Christ in a way that changes everything. And then we'll say with conviction that our fears led to a blessing.

Lord, when I am fearful, may my first instinct be to turn to You. When I experience anxiety, cause it to drive me straight into Your arms and deepen my relationship with You.

33

The Spirit helps us
with our weakness.
We do not know how
to pray as we should.
But the Spirit himself
speaks to God for us,
even begs God for us
with deep feelings that
words cannot explain.

ROMANS 8:26 NCV

*H*ave you ever felt so down you didn't even know how to pray? Sometimes we find ourselves with the desire to pray but feel so overwhelmed that it's hard to know how. In times of loss, depression, anxiety, or constant stress, we can get so worn down that we don't have the words to express to God how we are feeling. The good news is that the Holy Spirit helps us in our prayer lives. The third person of the Trinity never lacks words and knows exactly what we need from the Father. When we are too weak to approach the throne with confidence, we can take comfort in the fact that the Holy Spirit is praying on our behalf. The Spirit will direct our prayer lives so we pray in alignment with God's will. We don't have to be eloquent in our speech. God hears our cries, groans, and even the whispers that say, "Lord, help me."

> *Father, there are times when I am so weary I don't know how to pray. Thank You that the Holy Spirit prays on my behalf and You hear me even when my prayers lack clarity and eloquence.*

34

That's why I take
pleasure in my
weaknesses, and in
the insults, hardships,
persecutions, and
troubles that I suffer for
Christ. For when I am
weak, then I am strong.

2 CORINTHIANS 12:10 NLT

*T*oday's culture places a high value on the concept of independence and self-reliance. We encourage one another by saying things like, "You've got this." In our society, weakness is viewed as a liability, and people often say, "Only the strong survive." The problem with this way of thinking is it's at odds with what the Bible teaches. The Scriptures teach that all human beings have a sin problem we can't fix. As we live our lives in a fallen world, we will be habitually confronted with problems that are too much for us. The gospel calls us to a new way of thinking. As Christians, we must rely on Christ's power to address our sin problem and the way we fall short in everyday life. In our areas of weakness, we are to live by faith in Christ's power. Then, like Paul, we can say, "For when I am weak, then I am strong."

> *Lord, I pray I will rely on Your power and not my own limited strength. Teach me to turn my weaknesses into prayer requests and to trust in Your strength to meet my every need.*

35

I can do all things
through Christ who
strengthens me.

PHILIPPIANS 4:13 NIV

*T*he apostle Paul wrote the book of Philippians while he was in prison for preaching the gospel. Interestingly, his letter to the church at Philippi has much to say about joy and finding contentment in any situation (4:11). Because of his vibrant relationship with Christ, Paul was able to write from a filthy prison cell, "I can do all things through Christ who strengthens me." This promise doesn't mean that God will bless every endeavor we attempt.[6] Rather, when we study these words in the context of Paul's letter, it means that if we entrust ourselves to God and find our contentment in Christ, He will give us the strength to endure any situation. God will not leave us without the resources to do what He asks of us. As we find our contentment in Christ, we will find that God strengthens us to fulfill our callings and finish the work He assigns us.

> *Lord, I confess I have sought contentment from the world and found it didn't satisfy. I will seek and find contentment in You as You equip me with provision for every circumstance.*

36

"I know the plans I have for you, declares the LORD, plans for welfare and not for evil, to give you a future and a hope."

JEREMIAH 29:11 ESV

*W*hen the prophet Jeremiah wrote these words, he was writing to the Israelites, who were carried into exile from Jerusalem to Babylon and would ultimately spend seventy years in captivity (Jeremiah 29:4). This was a group of people who had their lives torn apart and had lost everything that was familiar to them. As exiles in a foreign land, they were undoubtedly shaken to the core and worried about their future. But God reassured them that their suffering would not last forever and that He had plans for their future. God is committed to redeeming His people and restoring us to wholeness. God kept His word to the Israelites; the exiles returned, and the nation of Israel was indeed restored for a time. Regardless of harrowing situations we might find ourselves in, we can trust that God is faithful to keep His word.

Father, as I seek Your will for my life, please make my path clear. Guide me in the way that You have planned for me, and equip me to fulfill my calling.

37

Be strong in the Lord
and in the strength of
His might. Put on the
full armor of God, so
that you will be able to
stand firm against the
schemes of the devil.

EPHESIANS 6:10–11 NASB

*A*s we go about our day-to-day business, it's easy to forget we have an Enemy who is committed to our destruction. God has a good plan for our lives, but the Enemy has a plan that, if carried out, would devastate us. Jesus said, "The thief comes only to steal and kill and destroy; I have come that they may have life, and have it to the full" (John 10:10 NIV). While it's true that Satan is too powerful for us to fight on our own, he is no match for God. Thankfully, the Lord hasn't left us on our own to fight against the schemes of the Devil. The apostle Paul instructed believers to "put on the full armor of God" (Ephesians 6:11) so we will be able to stand up to the Enemy. We would be foolish to attempt to fight the principalities of darkness in our own strength (2 Corinthians 10:4). But God has given us the resources we need to stand against the Devil.

> *Lord, I will be mindful of the Devil's schemes. Please protect me from the Enemy, and teach me to use the armor You have given me to stand against his wicked tactics.*

38

Whoever dwells in the
shelter of the Most High
will rest in the shadow
of the Almighty.
I will say of the LORD,
"He is my refuge
and my fortress,
my God, in whom
I trust."

PSALM 91:1–2 NIV

*I*t doesn't take more than a casual glance at the evening news to know that we live in a world where bad things happen. The perils of modern society are different from the dangers the writers of the Old Testament faced, but the refuge of the people of God remains the same. Although the author of Psalm 91 is anonymous, it's clear the topic of personal safety was at the forefront of the writer's mind. In times of peril, we all want a safe place to turn. The psalmist said, "Whoever dwells in the shelter of the Most High will rest in the shadow of the Almighty." To "dwell" means to stay somewhere on a continual basis. It's never too late to have a close relationship with God, and we have the opportunity to "dwell" in His presence. As believers, if we are careful to cultivate a relationship with God when things are going well, we will experience peace in His presence during times of trouble.

> *Father, please give me a continual sense of Your presence. Help me to cultivate a relationship with You that is personal and loving in both good times and during seasons of trouble.*

39

Fear of man will
prove to be a snare,
but whoever trusts in
the Lᴏʀᴅ is kept safe.

PROVERBS 29:25 NIV

*I*n the Scriptures, the term *fear* sometimes refers to *reverence*, and other times it denotes "trembling or terror." In Proverbs 29, the author was referring to the latter and communicated that being scared of other human beings is a snare for God's people. When believers are fearful of another person, it's likely the individual will have a measure of control over us. But if we trust God, there is no reason to fear anyone or anything, because "whoever trusts in the LORD is kept safe" (v. 25). The word *safe* used in this instance means "to be set inaccessibly high," meaning that God lifts us to a place of safety that is out of reach from human threats. Chronic fear of another person demonstrates a lack of faith that God will protect us, but God demonstrates time and again He is worthy of our trust.

Father, help me to remember that You are for me and, therefore, there is no reason to fear other people. I will revere You above all people and all things.

40

The only temptation that has come to you is that which everyone has. But you can trust God, who will not permit you to be tempted more than you can stand. But when you are tempted, he will also give you a way to escape so that you will be able to stand it.

1 CORINTHIANS 10:13 NCV

*W*e all experience temptation. God is not the source of our temptation, but He does permit us to experience it (James 1:13–14). Temptation isn't sin, but we will need God's help to confront temptation in a way that doesn't result in sin. In Paul's letter to the church at Corinth, he assured his readers that they shouldn't be surprised by temptation because it is universal. God won't permit us to be tempted beyond what we can bear, and He provides us a way to endure it. Scripture memory is one of the most effective tools in dealing with temptation. If we are confronted with a constant temptation in a specific area, it's wise to memorize scriptures that address the issue. The Bible teaches that with God's help we can defeat temptation.

> *Father, I do not want to succumb to sin. When I am tempted, provide me with discernment, and give me strength to choose obedience over sin.*

41

I will both lie down in
peace, and sleep;
For You alone, O Lᴏʀᴅ,
make me dwell in safety.

PSALM 4:8

*C*hronic insomnia is often associated with high levels of stress, worry, and anxiety. A lack of sleep can cloud our thinking, lower our immune system, and diminish quality of life. When King David penned Psalm 4, he was experiencing a season of troubling circumstances, but he wrote, "The LORD will hear when I call to him" (v. 3). Despite David's stressful conditions, he was able to go to bed and sleep because he took his problems to God in prayer, and then he trusted God would keep him safe. As long as we are in this world, we will be habitually confronted with problems we can't control. If we aren't careful, those problems have the potential to get the best of us and even affect our health and sleep patterns. As believers, we know that nothing is outside of God's control, so we can choose to trust God and experience His peace.

> *Father, teach me to deal with stress in healthy ways. I ask for plentiful sleep and help in making choices that are good for my mental, physical, and spiritual health.*

42

But those who wait
on the LORD
Shall renew their
strength;
They shall mount up
with wings like eagles,
They shall run and
not be weary,
They shall walk
and not faint.

ISAIAH 40:31

*C*hronic stress drains our strength. When we are running on empty, it might seem as if we will never feel revived and full of energy again. But the prophet Isaiah wrote that if God's people will place their hope in the Lord, their strength will be renewed. There is a vast difference between placing our hope in a fickle set of circumstances and placing our hope in God. To hope in the Lord means to wait with eager expectation that God will bring His promises to pass. God's Word is not fickle; it can be counted on. As we wait for God's promises to come to pass, the Word revives us. The words of Scripture are described as "alive and active," and they have the ability to penetrate "soul and spirit, joints and marrow" (Hebrews 4:12 NIV). God's Word revives us in a way that we will "run and not be weary," and we will "walk and not faint" (Isaiah 40:31).

Lord, when I am weary, revive me with Your Word. Give me rest when I am fatigued and refreshment when I am running on empty.

43

My flesh and my
heart fail;
But God is the strength
of my heart and my
portion forever.

PSALM 73:26

Many of us care deeply about our physical health, and we should; we need to take good care of our bodies. But the reality is, a time will come when our physical bodies will fail us. Our bodies are a gift from God, but they weren't made to last forever. Our relationship with God, on the other hand, can last for eternity. When the psalmist Asaph wrote Psalm 73, he communicated that God's strength would carry him when his own physical body failed. In this life, it's easy to place all our emphasis on what makes us comfortable here and now. But we must avoid spending all our time and energy on temporary things and ignoring what is eternal. And when we experience poor health, it's wise to remember that our suffering won't last forever, but we will be able to enjoy our relationship with God for eternity.

Father, as I take good care of my physical body, I will be quick to remember my spiritual life will last for eternity. Teach me to balance my time and effort accordingly.

44

The sufferings we
have now are nothing
compared to the
great glory that will
be shown to us.

ROMANS 8:18 NCV

The apostle Paul suffered more than most. According to Scripture, he endured multiple beatings, was stoned, shipwrecked, lost at sea, always on the move, subjected to various dangers, sleepless, hungry, cold, and naked, and he faced the daily concern for the churches he planted (2 Corinthians 11:25–29). Also, we know Paul was imprisoned for preaching the gospel (Philippians 1:14) and ultimately put to death for his faith. Yet Paul was confident that the suffering he experienced was a dim comparison to the glory that awaits believers in Christ Jesus. It's true that suffering in this life can be difficult. But for Christians, this life is not all there is to anticipate. We can be encouraged because a time is coming when all suffering will be over. Then the glory revealed to us will make our heartaches in this life seem like nothing compared to the joy we will experience.

Lord, in times of suffering help me to remember that all hard seasons will come to an end. I know that my best days await me in heaven.

45

Now we see things
imperfectly, like puzzling
reflections in a mirror,
but then we will see
everything with perfect
clarity. All that I know now
is partial and incomplete,
but then I will know
everything completely,
just as God now knows
me completely.

1 CORINTHIANS 13:12 NLT

*T*here are some questions we won't have answers to in this lifetime. In Paul's letter to the church at Corinth, he addressed this issue by using the analogy of a mirror. In Paul's era, mirrors were made from ancient metals, such as bronze, and a person's reflection was even dimmer than in a modern mirror.[7] Spiritually speaking, even with the Word of God and the Holy Spirit to teach us, we are still incapable of seeing and knowing some things in this lifetime. But when we enter into Christ's presence, and we see Him face-to-face, we will have complete understanding. Until then, we can trust in God's goodness and faithfulness. We don't have to have all the answers to know that God is for us and never against us (Romans 8:31), and we serve a God who loved us enough to die for us (5:8).

Father, permit me to know as much about You as You will allow. In the things that You withhold, please give me faith in Your goodness and righteousness.

46

"Therefore do not
be anxious about
tomorrow, for tomorrow
will be anxious for itself.
Sufficient for the day
is its own trouble."

MATTHEW 6:34 ESV

We've all heard the old saying, "One day at a time." Although the phrase has become cliché, it still holds a lot of wisdom. God is faithful to give us the grace to get through whatever comes our way, but He doesn't supply it in advance. Often we worry about what might happen, and our fears never even come to pass. Other times we get anxious about what we might be facing weeks or months down the road. God gives us grace at the exact time we need it. Jesus instructs His followers to focus our thoughts on the present day and to trust that God will provide as we have need. That doesn't mean we shouldn't make reasonable plans for the future. But worrying about the future is courting disaster that may never come. And even if we do face trouble in the future, God will help us at our exact time of need.

Father, I pray for grace to meet my needs today. Teach me not to worry about next week or next year. Help me to remember that Your grace will arrive at the time I need it.

47

Consider it pure joy, my
brothers and sisters,
whenever you face
trials of many kinds,
because you know that
the testing of your faith
produces perseverance.
Let perseverance finish
its work so that you may
be mature and complete,
not lacking anything.

JAMES 1:2–4 NIV

$\mathcal{A}$t first glance it seems strange that James would instruct his readers to be joyful "whenever you face trials of many kinds." After all, why should we be happy when trouble comes? But James was referring to trouble that challenges our faith. It is during times of testing that our faith grows, and we increase in our ability to persevere. Simply put, trials mature our faith. During seasons of struggle we often draw closer to God, and as a result, we experience Him in a way we never would during a time of ease. Our trials are never wasted. God will always use our trials for our good and His glory. The joy James described isn't dependent on outward circumstances, but instead is fueled by the belief that God will keep His promises and bring good out of even the worst of circumstances.

> God, help me to see trials as an opportunity to draw closer to You and grow in my faith. May every challenge I face bring us in closer fellowship.

48

You have not received
a spirit of slavery
leading to fear again,
but you have received
a spirit of adoption as
sons by which we cry
out, "Abba! Father!"

ROMANS 8:15 NASB

*B*efore becoming children of God, the Bible teaches, we were slaves to sin (Romans 6:17–18). But when we trust Christ as our Savior and become children of God, we receive the Holy Spirit (Ephesians 1:13). One of the roles of the Holy Spirit is to assure us that we are indeed children of God (Romans 8:16). As children of God, we have the privilege of calling the Father *Abba*. The term *Abba* is an informal Aramaic term for "Father" and is the equivalent of the English word *Daddy*. *Abba* is a name that denotes intimacy, dependence, and a lack of fear and anxiety.[8] In Christ, we are no longer slaves to sin, nor do we have to live in fear for one minute longer.

> *Father, I want my relationship with You to be be as close as a loving parent and dependent child. Help me to experience You as the perfect Father that You are.*

49

In all your ways
submit to him,
and he will make
your paths straight.

PROVERBS 3:6 NIV

If we aren't intentional about the way we live, there's a good chance we will wander aimlessly through the days, weeks, months, and years that weave together our life stories. If we have no clear goals, then it's impossible to know whether or not we are on track. The book of Proverbs offers a better way. The writer says that if we submit to God, He will make our paths straight. To submit to God means to acknowledge and obey Him in all areas of life. Proverbs teaches that if we submit to God, He will lead us in the right direction, and we will make continual progress toward our goal. None of us want to come to the end of our lives and realize we took the wrong path. Acknowledging God and obeying Him in everything we do allows us to follow as He leads us in the right direction.

Father, at the end of my life I want to have completed the work You have assigned me to do. Please teach me to make the best use of my time.

50

I have been crucified
with Christ and I no
longer live, but Christ
lives in me. The life I
now live in the body, I
live by faith in the Son
of God, who loved me
and gave himself for me.

GALATIANS 2:20 NIV

When we become Christ-followers, we quit living for our own desires and we intentionally "crucify" anything that doesn't align with God's will for our lives. We no longer live in our own strength, but by Christ's strength in us. Living this way is a game changer. Although our day-to-day responsibilities might look exactly the same, we can confront them with faith that God will supply everything we need rather than trying to figure out how we are going to make everything happen on our own. The apostle Paul reminded us on more than one occasion, "The righteous will live by faith" (Romans 1:17 NIV; Galatians 3:11 NIV). Jesus loved us enough to die for us, and therefore He can be trusted with every other detail in our lives. As we are faced with life's problems and the stress of everyday living, we can approach them in faith and rely on all the spiritual blessings and resources we have in Christ.

Father, empower me to die to everything that is not Your will for my life. Teach me to live my daily life by faith in Your Son.

51

Yea, though I walk
through the valley of
the shadow of death,
I will fear no evil;
For You are with me;
Your rod and Your staff,
they comfort me.

PSALM 23:4

When a child has a bad dream, it's not uncommon for him to run to his parents' room and wake them. The presence of a loving parent can calm a child when he is upset. As adults, when we experience troubling circumstances, we are sometimes tempted to put our best game face on and go it alone. But the Bible teaches that God's people never need to face life's challenges by themselves. When King David wrote Psalm 23, he acknowledged that he was walking through a dark valley. But David wasn't fearful, because he knew that God was with him, and His presence gave David comfort. When we are going through difficult times, we can be encouraged by staying mindful of God's presence. The Bible promises that God will never leave His children to fend for themselves: "Never will I leave you; never will I forsake you" (Hebrews 13:5 NIV).

Father, thank You for promising never to leave me. Help me to have a keen sense of Your presence, and teach me to rely on You during times of difficulty.

52

Do not lose the courage
you had in the past,
which has a great
reward. You must hold
on, so you can do what
God wants and receive
what he has promised.

HEBREWS 10:35–36 NCV

The Christian life calls for perseverance. The writer of the book of Hebrews urged his readers to keep pressing on. As Christ-followers, we are people of God's Word. That means we cling tightly to His promises. Our goal in this life is to fulfill God's will for our lives and to bring Him glory. That sounds simple enough, but the Christian life is full of hardships (Acts 14:22). Yet we are called to remain confident in the promises set before us. If we do, we will be richly rewarded (Hebrews 10:35 NIV). God keeps His promises. Jesus is who He says He is and will do as He said He would do. Our role is to have faith in the Son of God and live our lives in a way that demonstrates that Jesus will do exactly as He has said. Jesus is our confidence, and we persevere in the midst of hardships by placing our trust in Him.

Father, I pray I will resist the temptation to quit when times are hard. I ask You to fill me with perseverance. I pray You will empower me with endurance.

53

If God is for us, who
can ever be against us?

ROMANS 8:31 NLT

We can believe in the truth that God is for us and not against us (Psalm 56:9; Romans 8:31). By sending Christ to die for our sins, God went to the greatest of lengths to provide a way for us to be reconciled to Him. When we experience hard times, it's common to wonder if we've done something wrong. That may or may not be the case. The Bible makes it clear that God does discipline those He loves, but even discipline is intended for our good (Hebrews 12:6). Sometimes we go through hard times simply because we live in a fallen world. When we understand that God is fully committed to our good, we will be able to persevere during difficult times with increased endurance. God is a perfect and loving Father who desires for His children to flourish. Regardless of the situation, we must remember God is always for us.

Father, please settle in my heart and mind that You are for me and not against me. Help me to remember that You use difficult situations to increase my spiritual growth and maturity.

54

Lord, all my desire
is before You;
And my sighing is not
hidden from You.

PSALM 38:9

When King David wrote Psalm 38, he was suffering from the consequences of his sin (vv. 4–5), and he was afflicted with poor health and depression (vv. 7–8). David wasn't silenced by his suffering but instead poured out his complaints to God. While it's true the Bible warns about complaining and grumbling, it's always appropriate to process our feelings with God in prayer (Exodus 15–17; Numbers 11:1–11). Complaining to others demonstrates a lack of gratitude to God, and such complaining is usually directed at people who don't have the power to change our circumstances. Lamenting to God in prayer, on the other hand, is an intimate dialogue with our Creator. God is omniscient, meaning He is all-knowing, and He is aware of every problem we are dealing with. He is also omnipotent, meaning He has the power to change our situation. God knows our deepest fears, longings, and disappointments. Our prayer lives are the safest place to verbalize our heartaches.

> *Lord, help me to be quick to verbalize my frustrations in prayer. I ask for a transparent prayer life and that I will be comfortable sharing my deepest emotions with You.*

55

And God is able to
make all grace abound
to you, so that having
all sufficiency in all
things at all times,
you may abound in
every good work.

2 CORINTHIANS 9:8 ESV

$\mathcal{E}$ very good thing we possess is from God. Our material resources, health, skill sets, talents, spiritual gifts, and financial provision all come from Him. In his letter to the church at Corinth, the apostle Paul asked, "What do you have that you did not receive?" (1 Corinthians 4:7). The secular world teaches that we become rich by clinging to our wealth, but the Bible teaches we are blessed when we give. God blesses us, not so we can become rich by hoarding what He gives us, but so we can give freely. Our skills, talents, money, and spiritual gifts are intended to bless other people and build the kingdom of God. In God's economy, the more we give, the more blessed we become (Acts 20:35). God graciously replenishes the resources we give away, and He continuously blesses those who give so they continually have the means to keep giving. God blesses us so we can bless other people.

> Father, thank You for the countless ways You have blessed me and lavished me with Your grace. Teach me to be a vessel of Your goodness and bless others the way You have blessed me.

56

"Be still, and know
that I am God;
I will be exalted
among the nations,
I will be exalted
in the earth!"

PSALM 46:10

*G*od is faithful when everything around us is falling apart. Psalm 46 was likely written during the time God delivered Jerusalem from the Assyrians while King Hezekiah reigned (2 Kings 18–19; 2 Chronicles 32). In a time of crisis, the Jewish leaders had foolishly run to Egypt for help when they should have trusted God (Isaiah 30:1–2). God's instruction "Be still" literally means "Take your hands off" or "Relax."[9] His words were directed to the nations, but they can also apply to us as individuals. When things are falling apart, we prefer to act quickly on our own behalf. But our first step as Christ-followers should always be to seek God's protection and guidance. When we intervene apart from God's guidance, God sometimes allows us to get in situations that we can't get out of apart from His intervention so we will acknowledge His power and lordship over our lives.

> *Father, please give me wisdom to know when to act and when to wait. Forgive me for the times I have stepped outside Your will and looked for provision in other places.*

57

I know what it is to be in
need, and I know what
it is to have plenty. I
have learned the secret
of being content in any
and every situation,
whether well fed or
hungry, whether living
in plenty or in want.

PHILIPPIANS 4:12 NIV

*I*n a materialistic culture, it's easy to fall into the trap of always wanting the next thing. Or we might be deceived by thinking that if our circumstances were just the way we wanted, we would finally be happy. Paul teaches us otherwise. We'd be hard-pressed to find anyone in history who lived with more passion than the apostle Paul. His ministry subjected him to extreme circumstances on a regular basis, and yet he wrote to the church at Philippi, "I have learned the secret of being content in any and every situation." Contentment is not a result of ideal circumstances. Rather, contentment is a frame of mind that can only be found in Christ Jesus. Paul wrote, "I can do all this through him who gives me strength" (Philippians 4:13 NIV). Paul had learned that the key to contentment is not found in anything other than Jesus. But if we are content in Christ, no matter what situation we find ourselves in, we can experience His peace.

> *Father, help me remember that the contentment I am looking for can only be found in Jesus. I pray I will be content in Christ and all the blessings I have in Him.*

58

Keep me as the
apple of Your eye;
Hide me under the
shadow of Your wings.

PSALM 17:8

*H*ave you ever been in over your head? When King David wrote Psalm 17, he was surrounded by enemies who were trying to kill him. Although David was skilled in combat, he knew that if the Lord didn't intervene, he wouldn't survive (vv. 9, 11). David appealed to God and prayed, "Keep me as the apple of Your eye." The pupil is the "apple of the eye" and the most delicate part.[10] In the same way we protect the eye from injury, David was asking the Lord to protect him and shield him in the shadow of His wings. At times, regardless of our skills or experience, we will be in over our heads. Like David, we will be wise to call out to God for protection and provision. No matter what obstacles we are facing, God possesses the resources we lack and the provision we need.

Father, I sometimes find myself in situations that are too much for me to handle. It is then that You provide for me in ways I can't provide for myself. I ask for Your blessing, protection, and favor.

59

[The righteous] will have
no fear of bad news;
their hearts are
steadfast, trusting
in the Lord.

PSALM 112:7 NIV

*M*ost of us know a phone call can change our lives forever. We all know people who have been affected by accidents, diagnoses, and natural disasters. But as Christians, there is no need for us to live our day-to-day lives in fear of bad news. The psalmist described the righteous person as someone whose heart is set on the Lord and the confidence of His provision. Although we might not feel capable of facing whatever comes our way in our own strength, we can be encouraged that God will give us the grace we need to face each day. God doesn't dispense His grace to us in a onetime lifetime supply. He gives us grace to meet our daily needs as they arise. God is in control of every situation, and He will never allow anything to happen to us that is not ultimately for our good and His glory (Romans 8:28).

> *Father, I will not live in fear of bad news but in confidence of Your grace in every situation. Teach me to rely on You for my daily needs and seek You with all my heart.*

60

Everything that was
written in the past
was written to teach
us, so that through
the endurance taught
in the Scriptures and
the encouragement
they provide we
might have hope.

ROMANS 15:4 NIV

*T*he Word of God is a lifeline for every Christian. Paul instructed his readers that the Word of God will teach us as well as provide encouragement and hope. The psalmist wrote, "My soul is weary with sorrow; strengthen me according to your word" (Psalm 119:28 NIV). The Bible is the primary way God communicates with His people. As we read the Scriptures, we are taking in the message God intends to communicate (2 Timothy 3:16). He uses the Scriptures to increase our understanding, give us strength, correct us, and encourage us. As we approach the Scriptures, we will be wise to ask God to increase our understanding of His Word. Like the psalmist, we can pray, "Open my eyes that I may see wonderful things in your law" (Psalm 119:18 NIV). Reading God's Word is a privilege, and being a student of the Scriptures is something every believer in Christ can benefit from.

> *Father, please give me a deep love for Your Word. Reveal truth to me from Your Scriptures, and allow Your Word to be the guiding authority of my life.*

61

For am I now seeking
the favor of men, or of
God? Or am I striving
to please men? If I were
still trying to please
men, I would not be a
bond-servant of Christ.

GALATIANS 1:10 NASB

*A*re you a people pleaser? People pleasers go to extreme lengths to make everyone happy. The problem is, while it's relatively easy to make people happy, it's impossible to keep them happy. People pleasing is a full-time job with a dismal future. The apostle Paul wasn't a people pleaser; instead, he made it his aim to please God. In his letter to the church at Galatia, Paul addressed the issue of living either for God or man. In the Christian life, at times our faith calls us to be at odds with what is popular in modern culture. If we attempt to please other people to avoid ridicule or being disliked, then we are putting the opinion of man over the opinion of God. As Christians, we are called to be servants of Jesus Christ and to serve Him at any cost. That's why Paul wrote, "If I were still trying to please men, I would not be a bond-servant of Christ." The goal is not to please everyone; our motivation is to please God.

Father, please teach me how to be good to people without being consumed by what they think. Help me to remember I am to live for You and not the favor of people.

62

The righteous cry out,
and the LORD hears,
And delivers them out
of all their troubles.
The LORD is near to those
who have a broken heart,
And saves such as
have a contrite spirit.
Many are the afflictions
of the righteous,
But the LORD delivers
him out of them all.

PSALM 34:17–19

*I*t's frustrating to speak from the heart and not be heard. When other people ignore or disregard our words, it can be hurtful and discouraging. But the Bible makes it clear that God hears and responds to the prayers of His people. We may not feel as if anyone else is listening to us, but we can rest assured that God hears every word. Prayer is the most effective place to process our feelings, and when we pray, we have an audience with the God who can change our circumstances. When we are brokenhearted, we can be encouraged that God is close to those who are hurting, and He helps those with crushed spirits. We never have to suffer alone. God never promised us that we wouldn't have troubles. But in the midst of our troubles, we can be confident that God will see us through each one.

> *Lord, thank You for hearing my prayers. Bring changes to the areas in my life that need attention, and help me to trust that You are working in ways I don't see.*

63

My God will meet all
your needs according
to the riches of his
glory in Christ Jesus.

PHILIPPIANS 4:19 NIV

*G*od is faithful to meet the needs of His people. When Paul wrote his letter to the church at Philippi, he thanked them for the generosity they'd shown to meet his needs in ministry (Philippians 4:16). No other church had supported Paul the way the church at Philippi had, demonstrating a desire to support gospel ministry (v. 15). Everything we have has been given to us by God, and generosity to the kingdom of God is the only appropriate response. When we acknowledge that everything we have belongs to God and generously give back to support kingdom ministry and the needs of the poor and oppressed, we will find, like the Philippians, that God is generous and faithful to meet our needs. The phrase "according to the riches of his glory in Jesus Christ" reveals the extent to which God will go to provide for His people. God will provide everything we need to flourish.

> *Father, thank You for all the ways You have provided for my needs. All I have belongs to You, and I pray You will teach me to be a good steward of the resources You have given me.*

64

"Martha, Martha," the
Lord answered, "you
are worried and upset
about many things,
but few things are
needed—or indeed
only one. Mary has
chosen what is better,
and it will not be taken
away from her."

LUKE 10:41–42 NIV

*E*verything in our lives is affected by our relationship with Jesus. Mary and Martha were sisters who lived in the village of Bethany (John 11:1). When Jesus was traveling through town, they invited Him to their home. Martha was distracted by the chores that come with hospitality, but her sister, Mary, sat at Jesus' feet and listened to Him teach. When Martha complained to Jesus about her sister's behavior, Jesus defended Mary and told Martha that Mary had chosen what was "better" (Luke 10:42). Of course, hospitality and serving others are good things. Cooking, housekeeping, and entertaining guests are responsibilities that should be embraced. But Jesus pointed out that nothing is more important than our relationship with Him. If we neglect our relationship with Christ, we will miss the most important aspect of life. Our relationship with Jesus should be our number one priority. As we spend time with Jesus, He will equip and strengthen us to fulfill our responsibilities with enthusiasm.

> *Lord, You are my greatest treasure, and there is nothing more important than my relationship with You. Teach me to live every minute in light of this reality.*

65

"I told you these
things so that you
can have peace in
me. In this world you
will have trouble,
but be brave! I have
defeated the world."

JOHN 16:33 NCV

*E*ven though we know the world is full of problems, we are still sometimes surprised when trouble comes. Just before going to the cross, Jesus gathered His disciples and prepared them for what was about to take place. Jesus knew the disciples didn't understand what was about to happen and they would be fearful, confused, and anxious in the coming days. Jesus spoke to them so they would have peace. The Hebrew word *shalom*, which is translated "peace" here, is rich in meaning. It is not merely the absence of conflict but also denotes the peace that comes from having a right relationship with God.[11] It is a sense that all is well even in the midst of turmoil. Jesus' words to His disciples are important for us today. Even during times of conflict, we can experience the peace that comes from a right relationship with God.

> *Lord, help me not to be caught off guard or surprised when trouble comes. Troubles are part of living in a fallen world, but You are faithful in every circumstance.*

66

All praise to God, the
Father of our Lord Jesus
Christ. God is our merciful
Father and the source of
all comfort. He comforts
us in all our troubles
so that we can comfort
others. When they are
troubled, we will be able
to give them the same
comfort God has given us.

2 CORINTHIANS 1:3–4 NLT

*T*he apostle Paul suffered more than most. The Scriptures tell us he was beaten with rods, stoned, shipwrecked, adrift at sea, always on the move, confronted with various dangers, experienced sleepless nights, suffered without food and water, was subjected to harsh elements, and dealt with the daily stress and anxiety of pastoral leadership (2 Corinthians 11:25–28). But during his suffering, he experienced the Father's compassion and comfort. Our suffering as Christians is never wasted. Paul was a recipient of God's comfort during times of distress, but he knew God didn't intend for him to keep it to himself. God comforts us during times of trouble so we can comfort others. When we see other people struggling, it's our responsibility to help. The difficulties Paul faced increased his compassion for other people going through hard times. The same is true for us. If we are willing, God will use our times of affliction to mature us into people who effectively minister to others in the midst of hardship.

> *Father, please don't allow the suffering I've experienced to be wasted. Help me to comfort others in the same way You have comforted me during times of grief.*

133

67

It is the LORD who
goes before you. He
will be with you; he
will not leave you or
forsake you. Do not
fear or be dismayed.

DEUTERONOMY 31:8 ESV

*I*t's daunting when God calls us outside of our comfort zones. When God called Joshua to fill Moses' position of leadership, it must have been an overwhelming appointment. Joshua would be responsible for leading the Israelites into the promised land, and that was no small assignment. Undoubtedly the Israelites were anxious about their new leader and the task at hand. The Israelites would be conquering new territory as they moved into the promised land, and they must have experienced a fear of the unknown. But in today's verse Moses assured them that God would go before them, and He would be with them, so there was no need to be fearful or discouraged. In the same way, we are often fearful of new assignments and trying things we've never attempted before. But God is faithful to supply the grace we need to do the work He calls us to do. Like Joshua and the Israelites, we too can count on His presence and provision for everything we need.

> *Father, I will not be intimidated by new tasks but confident in Your grace. Help me to step out in faith into new areas that You call me and obey You in every thought, word, and deed.*

68

May your unfailing
love be my comfort,
according to your
promise to your servant.

PSALM 119:76 NIV

*L*ife is difficult, and during times of distress, God's people are called to rely heavily on His promises. In tough seasons, God's promises give us strength, encouragement, and hope for better days. Regardless of what we are going through, we can find comfort in God's love and His Word. The psalmist wrote, "May your unfailing love be my comfort." When we come upon hard times, we can pray the same way. The promises of God are a powerful way to frame our prayer lives, and we can be confident we are praying in alignment with God's will when we pray the Scriptures. God's promises are for all seasons of life, but we can find comfort by clinging to the Scriptures even more during times of trouble. Knowledge of God's love for us and faith in His promises will provide hope for our darkest days and remind us that better seasons are still to come.

Father, I look to the promises in Your Word with anticipation. Teach me to cling to Your promises and to rely on Your Word because You are faithful.

69

Sing, O heavens!
Be joyful, O earth!
And break out in
singing, O mountains!
For the LORD has
comforted His people,
And will have mercy
on His afflicted.

ISAIAH 49:13

*W*orship is a powerful expression of our love for God, and the Lord is worthy of all the glory we can give Him. Regardless of our circumstances, those of us who belong to Christ have good reason to worship Him every day for the rest of our lives. Because of what Jesus has done on our behalf, we are the most blessed people on the planet (Romans 5:8). Worship is not only appropriate to demonstrate our love and gratitude to God, but worship is also good for us. When we are feeling down or when we are confronted with a troubling circumstance, singing songs of worship shifts our focus away from our problem and redirects our gaze to the power and majesty of God. Worship stirs our faith and lifts our spirits. Singing songs of praise reminds us that God is in control, and no problem is too difficult for Him.

Father, I don't want my worship to be limited to Sunday services. Teach me to incorporate worship in my everyday life and to praise You every day of the week.

70

Therefore I will
look to the LORD;
I will wait for the God
of my salvation;
My God will hear me.

MICAH 7:7

$\mathcal{I}$t can be discouraging when we see other people making poor choices that harm themselves and other people. When the prophet Micah wrote these words, he was surrounded by unfaithful leaders who were behaving in an evil manner (Micah 7:3–4). Micah was so distressed by what he saw that he wrote, "Woe is me!" (v. 1). When we witness people living in rebellion against God and disregarding His mercy, it's heartbreaking to watch. But Micah resolved to be faithful to God in the midst of evil that was around him. Micah refused to participate. Instead, he wrote, "But as for me, I watch in hope for the LORD" (v. 7 NIV). Regardless of what is going on around us, we have the ability to choose our own way. Micah chose to wait for God, and he knew that God would hear his prayers. Although Micah began with a cry of mourning when he said, "Woe is me!" he ended with renewed confidence that God would act on his behalf (v. 20).

> *Father, regardless of what is going on around me, I pray I will be a faithful servant who obeys You. Empower me to commit myself to prayer for those who are far from You.*

71

I would have lost heart,

unless I had believed

That I would see the

goodness of the LORD

In the land of the living.

Wait on the LORD;

Be of good courage,

And He shall strengthen

your heart;

Wait, I say, on the LORD!

PSALM 27:13–14

*I*t's likely that David wrote Psalm 27 while he was waiting to become king of Israel. God had promised the throne to him, but a long series of taxing events took place before he became king (1 Samuel 16). For a time, David was exiled from his home while King Saul was hunting for him. Saul and his men were telling lies about David to damage his reputation and intended to physically harm or kill him (Psalm 27:2, 12). Even though David was in a stressful situation, he remained confident in the Lord. He was well aware of the threat he was facing, but he understood that the difficult season he was in would not last forever. When we remain close to God, He will equip us to overcome any fear or obstacle that comes our way. Like David, if we wait for the Lord, He will increase our strength and give us the grace to face the challenge.

> *Lord, teach me to place my confidence in You rather than my circumstances. Help me be quick to remember You are in control of all things and that hard seasons won't last forever.*

72

The God of peace
will soon crush Satan
under your feet. May
the grace of our Lord
Jesus be with you.

ROMANS 16:20 NLT

*S*atan has done an incalculable amount of damage to this world and the people in it, but his time is limited. A time is coming when believers will no longer be subjected to spiritual warfare and oppression from the Enemy. Paul encouraged his readers with the news, "The God of peace will soon crush Satan under your feet." Paul's analogy echoes Genesis 3:15. After the fall of man, God told the serpent that Christ would crush his head (NIV). As believers, we can be encouraged by the fact that Satan's reign of destruction will come to an end. Even though Satan has a degree of influence over our world right now, he is a defeated foe, and those of us in Christ do not need to fear. The apostle John wrote, "You, dear children, are from God and have overcome them, because the one who is in you is greater than the one who is in the world" (1 John 4:4 NIV).

> Lord, I will remain alert to the Enemy's schemes. Thank You that because of Jesus, I can live in expectation of Satan's final defeat and look forward to the time when he is no longer a threat.

73

"Ask, and it will be given
to you; seek, and you
will find; knock, and it
will be opened to you."

MATTHEW 7:7 ESV

*T*oo often, we use prayer as a last resort, but God intends for prayer to be our first response. Prayer is a spiritual discipline that we need to engage in daily. When we petition God with a prayer request, it's sometimes tempting to give up and quit praying when we don't get what we ask for right away. But the Bible teaches that we are to persevere in prayer (Luke 18:1–8). Some translations of today's verse render it, "Keep asking, . . . keep searching, . . . keep knocking" (HCSB). As believers, we can't expect to say a few half-hearted prayers and be surprised if our petitions aren't granted. It is a privilege to come into the Lord's presence and communicate with Him, and once we make it a regular habit, it will likely become the most joyful part of our day. God answers the prayers of His people, but we are called to devote ourselves to prayer (Colossians 4:2 NIV).

> *Lord, teach me to persevere in prayer and press on when I am tempted to quit. Help me to devote myself to prayer and enjoy a vibrant prayer life.*

74

When a man's ways
please the LORD,
He makes even his
enemies to be at
peace with him.

PROVERBS 16:7

*n*o matter how much we'd prefer to avoid it, there will be times when we are confronted with someone who doesn't like us. Unfortunately, some of us will even have enemies, and those enemies might have a measure of influence in our lives. But God is in control of all people, places, and circumstances. When we are walking in obedience to God's will for our lives, the Lord will open doors for us and make things happen that we never could bring to pass on our own. God can even cause our enemies to be at peace with us. Obeying God's will doesn't necessarily mean we will experience a life of ease— far from it. There will still be challenges. But when our way is pleasing to God, He will remove obstacles that stand in our way. There is no need for believers to invest time being overly concerned with those who dislike us or wish us harm. Our goal should be living a life that is pleasing to God and trusting Him to deal with our enemies.

> *Father, give me wisdom in my relationships, and teach me how to deal wisely with people. Please deal with my enemies, and empower me to live for You.*

75

The fruit of that
righteousness
will be peace;
its effect will be
quietness and
confidence forever.

ISAIAH 32:17 NIV

*G*od's people can have peace with the Father because of what Jesus has done on our behalf. The prophet Isaiah foresaw that there would be a coming Messiah and wrote, "See, a king will reign in righteousness and rulers will rule with justice" (Isaiah 32:1 NIV). In Jesus, we can be at peace with God because He has atoned for our sins and imputed His righteousness to all who believe in Him, and follow Him as Lord. Paul wrote, "God made him who had no sin to be sin for us, so that in him we might become the righteousness of God" (2 Corinthians 5:21 NIV). As we experience peace with God, through faith in Jesus Christ, we can live in peace in the midst of troubling circumstances. God takes full responsibility for His children, and because of His provision, we can live life in quiet confidence that He will do as He has promised.

> *Father, thank You that because of Christ's sacrifice on the cross, I am reconciled to You. I will live in peace knowing that my sins are forgiven and that I belong to You.*

76

Do not fret because
of those who are evil
or be envious of those
who do wrong.

PSALM 37:1 NIV

Watching evil unfold in the world is discouraging. Sometimes it's tempting to believe the evildoers are getting away with their behavior, but that's not true. God is a God of justice. David instructed his readers not to fret over the wrongdoing they observed or to be envious of those who do wrong and seemingly get away with it. Every sin ever committed in this world will one day be addressed by God. The one who sinned will be forgiven because the sin will be covered by the blood of Christ, or the one who sinned will be subjected to God's wrath. Solomon wrote in Ecclesiastes, "God will bring into judgment both the righteous and the wicked, for there will be a time for every activity, a time to judge every deed" (3:17 NIV). No one can outrun the consequences of evil behavior, and God will address all sin.

> Father, I know that You will deal with every evil and injustice. I pray my life will point other people to the righteousness of God in Christ.

77

Jesus stood up and
commanded the
wind and said to the
waves, "Quiet! Be
still!" Then the wind
stopped, and it became
completely calm.

MARK 4:39 NCV

Storms come in a variety of shapes and sizes. In day-to-day life, some of the most common offenders are financial issues, medical problems, depression and anxiety, tension at work, addiction, family disputes, and other problems that leave us feeling fearful and confused. In the gospel of Mark, we read an account of Jesus and His disciples encountering a storm as they traveled by boat. The disciples were terrified and feared for their lives, but Jesus was sound asleep in the boat. When they woke up Jesus, He rebuked the wind and calmed the storm. By doing so, Jesus demonstrated His power over nature. Jesus is not only in control of nature; He is also sovereign over every troubling circumstance we encounter. Like the disciples, we too can approach Jesus for help. The author of Hebrews wrote, "Let us then approach God's throne of grace with confidence, so that we may receive mercy and find grace to help us in our time of need" (4:16 NIV).

Lord, when things seem out of control, I know You are sovereign over every situation. Help me in times of trouble, and address the circumstances that are causing distress.

78

May the Lord of peace
himself give you his
peace at all times and
in every situation. The
Lord be with you all.

2 THESSALONIANS 3:16 NLT

*T*he world defines peace as a sense of calmness and tranquility that comes when everything is going well and conflict is absent. Of course, this type of peace is easily lost and shallow at best. The type of peace the Bible describes is completely different from the peace of this world. Spiritual peace is the settled confidence that we are reconciled to God because of our faith in Jesus Christ.[12] It is the knowledge that our sins are forgiven and that we have been given everything we need to live a godly life (2 Peter 1:3 NIV). The peace God offers to His people is not dependent on outward circumstances. Paul said we can experience God's peace "at all times and in every situation" (2 Thessalonians 3:16 NLT). The peace God gives can't be taken away and can be experienced during the most stressful seasons of life.

> *Lord, I know that nothing can change the fact that I belong to You. I pray that regardless of what is happening, I will experience a strong sense of Your peace and joy in my salvation.*

79

To us a child is born,
to us a son is given,
and the government will
be on his shoulders.
And he will be called
Wonderful Counselor,
Mighty God,
Everlasting Father,
Prince of Peace.

ISAIAH 9:6 NIV

*J*esus is a divine gift to sinners. Apart from Christ, we all would have perished in sin because all people have fallen short of the glory of God (Romans 3:23). But in His mercy, God sent Jesus to save sinners and provide a way for us to be reconciled to the Father. In our culture, many people believe there are multiple paths to God, but the Bible teaches that is not true. Jesus said, "I am the way and the truth and the life. No one comes to the Father except through me" (John 14:6 NIV). Jesus is our only hope for salvation, and Jesus alone has the ability to hold our lives together (Acts 4:12; Colossians 1:17 NIV). Jesus is worthy of all of our honor and praise. He is the greatest treasure we possess, and He is the answer to our every question. Everything in life rises and falls on our relationship with Jesus. He is everything.

Jesus, I acknowledge that You are the only path to salvation. Thank You for making a way for me to be reconciled to the Father and for securing eternal life on my behalf.

80

"The thief does not come except to steal, and to kill, and to destroy; I have come that they may have life, and that they may have it more abundantly."

JOHN 10:10

*S*atan's goal is to steal, kill, and destroy the things we hold most dear. As Christ-followers, we must be mindful that we have an Enemy who is committed to our destruction. While the Enemy's goal is to destroy us, Jesus came so we would have abundant life. Jesus' mission for coming to this world was to save the lost (Luke 19:10). Thankfully, we don't have to wait to get to heaven before we experience abundant life in His name. Abundant living is for the here and now. Our time in this world is limited, and we should be mindful to invest it wisely. Jesus intends for us to thrive and live productive lives that bear fruit for the kingdom of God. Abiding in Jesus is the key to bearing fruit because apart from Him we can do nothing (John 15:5 NIV). In Christ, we are empowered to live productive lives that bring glory to God and joy to us.

> *Lord, I pray I will enjoy the abundant life You to intend for me to have. Give me wisdom to know how to live well and use my time wisely.*

81

It is God who arms
me with strength,
And makes my
way perfect.
He makes my feet like
the feet of deer,
And sets me on
my high places.

PSALM 18:32–33

*A*fter a long and challenging season of being hunted by King Saul, David experienced God's rescue. Undoubtedly, he was delighted and relieved. David had survived despite a group of enemies who wanted to take his life before he could ascend the throne of Israel (Psalm 18:17). He didn't take any credit for surviving the ordeal but acknowledged that it was God who kept him safe. David knew it was God who had given him the strength to endure, and he knew God had protected him. Hopefully, most of us will never face such a dangerous situation, but we will all go through trials. David's words offer both encouragement and instruction. We can be encouraged knowing that our trials will not last forever; they will come to an end. And if we are wise, we will respond as David did and give God the credit He is due.

> *Lord, please protect me and bring me through every trial. Thank You for all the ways You act on my behalf. I pray for Your counsel, favor, and guidance.*

82

The LORD lift up His
countenance upon you,
And give you peace.

NUMBERS 6:26

$\mathcal{W}$e often seek God's hand, and we should, because the Bible encourages us to do so; He is the provider of all things (1 Corinthians 4:7). But how often do we seek His face? As Christ-followers, we have the jaw-dropping privilege of communing with our God, the Creator of the universe. While there's nothing wrong with seeking God's hand, we cut our relationship short if we don't pursue an intimate relationship with the Lord that goes far deeper than materialistic needs. King David wrote, "You have said, 'Seek my face.' My heart says to you, Your face, LORD, do I seek" (Psalm 27:8 ESV). If we draw near to God, we can rest assured that He will draw near to us (James 4:8). As believers, we have the opportunity to experience a day-to-day relationship with the Lord that will be the source of our greatest joy. In the context of that relationship, we will experience His peace.

> *Lord, I will seek Your face all the days of my life. Help my relationship with You to flourish and grow deeper with each passing year. Teach me to love and value You above all things.*

83

Jesus Christ is the
same yesterday,
today, and forever.

HEBREWS 13:8 NCV

*S*ometimes things in life change so quickly we feel as if the rug has been pulled out from under our feet. We've all experienced relationships that have come and gone, job changes, moves, and the inevitable transitions that come with growing older each year. Thankfully, the Scriptures teach that Jesus never changes. The writer of Hebrews penned, "Jesus Christ is the same yesterday, today, and forever." When we study the Scriptures and grow in the knowledge of Christ's attributes, His character, and His ways, we can trust that He will deal with us in the same way He is represented in the Bible. Few things remain the same, but we can take comfort in the fact that Jesus never changes. Jesus is forever faithful, trustworthy, and steadfast in His love for us. Everything around us might change in an instant, but we can count on Jesus eternally.

Jesus, thank You for never changing and for continuing to be my constant source of security. Lord, even when things around me fall apart, You remain steadfast and faithful.

84

With You is the
fountain of life;
In Your light we
see light.

PSALM 36:9

*H*ave you ever been in a pitch-black room or driven on a country road so dark you can't see any farther than the headlights? Unsettling, isn't it? For most of us darkness represents the unknown or something sinister. Throughout the Scriptures, light and darkness are used as metaphors to represent the goodness of God and the evil that is in the world. David prayed to God, "For with You is the fountain of life; in Your light we see light." When we are confronted with evil or facing an uncertain future, we can be confident that God will show us the way. The apostle John described Jesus this way: "In him was life, and that life was the light of all mankind. The light shines in the darkness, and the darkness has not overcome it" (John 1:4–5 NIV). Although darkness is prevalent in some places, we can rest assured that it won't prevail because the light of God has overcome the darkness.

> *Jesus, thank You for overcoming the darkness in this fallen world. Help me to be a light that points people to Jesus Christ and the saving work of His redemption.*

85

"Surely I am with you
always to the very
end of the age."

MATTHEW 28:20 NIV

When Jesus issued the Great Commission to His followers, He said, "Go therefore and make disciples of all nations, baptizing them in the name of the Father and of the Son and of the Holy Spirit," and He promised His presence would remain with them wherever they went (Matthew 28:19–20). Jesus is called "Immanuel," which means "God with us." Jesus is present not only when His people gather for worship but also when we scatter into the world as His witnesses. During Jesus' earthly ministry, He could only be in one place at a time because when He took on flesh, He subjected Himself to the natural laws of the universe. But since His resurrection and ascension, He is omnipresent through the Spirit. Regardless of where we are or how far we travel, we can trust that Christ is with us.

Lord, thank You for being continually present with Your people. Teach me to rest in the knowledge that I am secure in Your presence and I will never be left to go it alone.

86

We know that if the
earthly tent we live
in is destroyed, we
have a building from
God, an eternal house
in heaven, not built
by human hands.

2 CORINTHIANS 5:1 NIV

*A*s the apostle Paul grew older, it would have been easy for him to tone down his preaching and avoid the topics that stirred the ire of his enemies. But Paul wasn't afraid of death because he was anticipating heaven. Paul understood death was inevitable, and while he was alive he was committed to investing his life in serving Christ. That's why he could write, "For to me, to live is Christ, and to die is gain" (Philippians 1:21). It's tempting to live with a self-preserving notion that avoids taking risks for the gospel, but the New Testament saints knew of no such attitude. As Christians, we must be mindful that our time in this world will come to an end. While it's true that it's wise for us to take good care of ourselves, the end goal of the Christian life isn't self-preservation, but a life that is pleasing to God.

> *Lord, teach me how to live a full life all my days on this earth and to use my time wisely. I will have no fear of death but will anticipate what awaits me in heaven.*

87

Great peace have those
who love Your law,
And nothing causes
them to stumble.

PSALM 119:165

*T*here are a lot of great books to read, but the Word of God differs from all other books. The Scriptures are God's Word to humankind and are intended to teach, rebuke, correct, and train in righteousness (2 Timothy 3:16 NIV). For Christ-followers, the Word of God is our final authority. The Bible teaches us about God, His plan of salvation, and how to live as a Christian. It's impossible to know God and walk in obedience to Him apart from being a student of the Scriptures. The book of Hebrews describes the Word of God as "living and powerful" (4:12). When we spend time studying the Scriptures, we increase in wisdom and learn the way God intends for us to live. As we lean on the promises of God, we experience peace. Nothing can make us stumble because, as we rely on God's guidance, He leads the way.

Father, I commit myself to being a student of Your Word. As I study, I pray that Your Word will change me and make me more like Jesus.

88

Set your mind on the
things above, not on the
things that are on earth.

COLOSSIANS 3:2 NASB

*T*he apostle Paul understood how vital our thought life is, and he spoke of it often. He said to the Colossians, "Set your mind on the things above, not on the things that are on earth" (3:2 NASB). The phrase "set your mind" suggests that we can and should be intentional about what we think about. It's life changing when we realize we have the ability to reject destructive thoughts that produce anxiety and replace them with thoughts that are helpful and true. One of the primary ways we can set our minds on the things above is to meditate on the promises of God. We do this by identifying passages from Scripture that apply to our circumstances and thinking about these promises. When a thought comes that tempts us to worry, we can be ready to interrupt it with the truth of God's Word. If we focus on the promises of God, our thoughts will shift from fear to faith.

> *Father, please teach me to manage my thoughts. Help me to set my mind on things above and to cultivate a godly thought life.*

89

Be of good courage,
And He shall strengthen
your heart,
All you who hope
in the Lord.

PSALM 31:24

*M*y heart's not in it anymore." This common saying signals that someone has disengaged or lost interest in something that once was important to him or her. Perhaps you've said it yourself. Sometimes we get worn down by fear, worry, and challenging circumstances. Negative factors can affect our motivation and reduce our desire to keep pressing on. The psalmist encouraged his readers, "Be of good courage, and He shall strengthen your heart." God can change our hearts and improve our thinking. When we are worn-out, He has the resources to refresh us. If we place our hope in God, He will increase our strength, motivate our wills, and empower us to accomplish everything He has called us to do. When we are feeling faint of heart, we don't have to stay that way. God will increase our strength.

Father, Your Word says You never grow tired or weak. Please empower me with Your strength and perseverance, and equip me to do everything You have called me to do.

90

"I am the Alpha and
the Omega, the First
and the Last, the
Beginning and the End."

REVELATION 22:13 NCV

*T*he original recipients of the book of Revelation spoke Greek, so Jesus identified Himself as the Alpha and the Omega, which are the first and last letters of the Greek alphabet.[13] The threefold description of Jesus as "the Alpha and the Omega," "the First and the Last," and "the Beginning and the End" in today's verse illustrates that there has never been a time when Jesus didn't exist—and that He will exist for eternity. Jesus is the source of all things, and He is infinite. As followers of Christ, we can be encouraged that His power is limitless; He can certainly handle what discourages you today. Jesus is far more than a teacher, rabbi, or great prophet. Jesus is the Son of God and the second person of the Trinity. Bringing glory to Christ's unmatched identity should be the goal of every believer.

Jesus, I give You praise and glory, for You are the Alpha and the Omega and everything in between. Your power is limitless, and there is nothing too hard for You.

91

"And I will ask the
Father, and he will
give you another
Advocate, who will
never leave you."

JOHN 14:16 NLT

*J*ust before going to the cross, Jesus had a conversation with His disciples to prepare them for what life would be like after His death and resurrection. The disciples didn't understand what was about to take place at Calvary and were shaken at the prospect of the looming events. They had enjoyed His physical presence for more than three years, and they would undoubtedly grieve His absence. They had left homes and businesses and risked their lives and reputations to follow Jesus, and now things seemed to be coming apart at the seams. But Jesus reassured them and promised that "another Advocate," the Holy Spirit, would be with them and all future believers. Among other things, the Holy Spirit teaches, guides, strengthens, and intercedes on behalf of believers. The Bible teaches that the Spirit dwells in every believer in Jesus Christ. Like the disciples, there are times we feel uncertain about the future, but we can be confident that the Holy Spirit is always with us.

> *Father, teach me to be mindful of the Spirit's indwelling in me, and help me to be quick to obey and follow His counsel.*

92

"Blessed are the poor in spirit, for theirs is the kingdom of heaven."

MATTHEW 5:3 ESV

*O*ur culture puts a high premium on self-reliance, self-confidence, and independence. But in Jesus' Sermon on the Mount, he said, "Blessed are the poor in spirit, for theirs is the kingdom of heaven." What does it mean to be "poor in spirit"? It means to place our confidence in God rather than ourselves.[14] To be "poor in spirit" means to make an accurate assessment of ourselves and see that apart from God we aren't capable of anything (John 15:5). Until we are "poor in spirit," we will view our relationship with God as nothing more than a self-improvement program, but that's not the gospel of Jesus Christ. As we spend time in God's Word and understand His holiness and our sinfulness, we will realize that apart from Christ's intervention we are doomed to failure. In Christ, however, we can live with all the confidence in the world.

Lord, I place no confidence in my flesh, but I am exceedingly confident in You. Teach me to abandon self-reliance and to depend whole-heartedly on You.

93

The angel of the Lord
encamps all around
those who fear Him,
And delivers them.

PSALM 34:7

King David wrote Psalm 34 after a dangerous experience he had in Gath with the Philistines (1 Samuel 21:10–22:1). David's enemies were pursuing him, and he and his family were forced to flee to a cave because they feared for their lives. Those enemies had repeatedly chased David, so he could say from experience that God had been faithful to keep him safe. Our enemies, obstacles, and setbacks might be too much for us, but they are not beyond God's control. David recognized that he hadn't escaped the hands of his enemies because of his own strength, wisdom, or strategy. He was still alive because God had protected him. He knew that God had delivered him and that he could take no credit for his own rescue. God protects those who revere His name, and He delivers us from people and situations that are too much for us.

Father, even in the midst of dangerous times, You are faithful to protect Your people. Deliver me from dangerous people and situations, and keep me safe in Your loving care.

94

Devote yourselves to
prayer, being watchful
and thankful.

COLOSSIANS 4:2 NIV

*O*ne theologian has said, "I have yet to meet a chronic worrier who enjoys an excellent prayer life."[15] What might our lives look like if we invested our time in prayer rather than wasting time worrying? The apostle Paul knew how important our prayer lives are, and he instructed his readers, "Devote yourself to prayer." To devote ourselves means to give our time and full attention. When we devote ourselves to something, it's not a casual or occasional endeavor but a routine commitment. Paul taught that prayer is to be a consistent spiritual discipline in the Christian life. Prayer is the way we fellowship with God and offer praise, thanks, and gratitude, as well as how we petition Him for our needs. Through the process of prayer, God strengthens us to meet the demands of life (Matthew 26:36–46). When we neglect prayer, we are weak and unprepared to face our problems. But if we will devote ourselves to prayer, God will strengthen us for every task.

> *Lord, in the Scriptures You modeled what it looked like to have a committed prayer life. Please help me to make prayer a priority, and teach me to devote myself to it.*

95

He is not here;
he has risen!

LUKE 24:6 NIV

The incomparable power of God was evident when onlookers peered into the empty tomb. The women who had gone to the tomb that morning to deliver spices they had prepared were stunned by the news of Christ's resurrection. But two men "in clothes that gleamed like lightning" asked, "Why do you look for the living among the dead?" (Luke 24:4–5 NIV). Christ's death and resurrection demonstrated that He has power over even death (2 Timothy 1:10). As Christ-followers, we can be encouraged that there is no problem or principality more powerful than Jesus. Amazingly, that same power lives in every believer in Jesus Christ. The apostle Paul wrote, "If the Spirit of Him who raised Jesus from the dead dwells in you, He who raised Christ from the dead will also give life to your mortal bodies through His Spirit who dwells in you" (Romans 8:11).

> *Father, the Scriptures demonstrate that You have power over death. There is nothing in my life that is too difficult for You. I pray You will demonstrate Your authority in every aspect of my life.*

96

But He knows the
way that I take;
When He has tested
me, I shall come
forth as gold.

JOB 23:10

*P*roblems have the potential to destroy us or make us stronger. We've all met people who have experienced trials and become bitter toward God and have stayed stuck in the past. Other people who struggle through tough times come through with a closer relationship with God and a deeper faith. Job was one of those people. Job lost his family, home, health, and a vast sum of resources, but he still didn't become bitter with God. Although Job experienced dark days that challenged his faith, he endured his suffering and came through with his faith intact. Trials purify our faith because they force us to decide what we really believe about God. The fire of affliction removes the impurities that linger in our spiritual lives. Job's faith went through the fire, but he came "forth as gold." As we go through challenging seasons, we should remember to ask God to increase our faith and allow our seasons of testing to make us stronger.

> *Lord, I pray that my problems will not make me bitter but that they will bring me closer to You. Allow the troubles I face to embolden my faith and increase my trust in You.*

97

It is good that one
should hope and
wait quietly
For the salvation
of the Lord.

LAMENTATIONS 3:26

*n*one of us enjoy waiting, but God often calls His people to wait for Him to act. The writer of Lamentations 3 had experienced a season of affliction but continued to rely on God's love and mercy (vv. 1–22). Although it probably seemed as if his suffering would never come to an end, the writer resolved to "wait quietly for the salvation of the LORD." In this context, the "salvation of the LORD" refers to deliverance from peril, rather than salvation from sin.[16] As he waited, he recalled God's goodness, mercy, and love. As we wait for God to act, it's helpful to remember the ways God has worked on our behalf in the past. Recognizing how God has been faithful to us stirs our faith and increases our trust that He will do the same in the future.

Lord, I ask for discernment to know when it's wise to wait and when it's time to act. Help me to be obedient to Your timing and not act out of alignment with Your will.

98

Blessed is the man who
endures temptation;
for when he has been
approved, he will
receive the crown of
life which the Lord
has promised to those
who love Him.

JAMES 1:12

*W*hen our faith is tested, we will either give up or persevere. Testing is never enjoyable, but it does produce perseverance. Anything worthwhile in life calls for perseverance, and our spiritual lives are no exception. Our faith will never become stronger unless we are confronted with obstacles that cause us to exercise it. James went as far as to say we are blessed when we persevere under trial because those who persevere will receive the "crown of life." James's words serve to encourage his readers to endure trials with faith so that they might receive the reward God has promised. Although rewards shouldn't be our primary motivation in serving God, they can motivate us during trials and testing and help us maintain focus.

> *Lord, I recognize that the Christian life calls for endurance. Please give me the strength I need to persevere. Empower me to keep going when I am tired, and give me an attitude that refuses to give up.*

99

Let the peace of Christ
rule in your hearts, since
as members of one
body you were called to
peace. And be thankful.

COLOSSIANS 3:15 NIV

*G*ratitude is a hallmark of all believers in Jesus Christ because it is a natural and appropriate response to everything God has done on our behalf. Being thankful is also necessary for maintaining a peaceful heart. When we are thankful, our focus is directed to all the ways God has blessed us and the ways He continues to work on our behalf. On the other hand, when we are ungrateful, we tend to focus on what we lack. When we fail to be thankful, we neglect to acknowledge all the ways God has blessed us, and inevitably we will lose our peace and experience a lack of contentment. Thankfulness directs our thoughts to what is right in our world, while a lack of gratitude emphasizes everything we think should be different. Paul instructed his readers to "be thankful" because we are "called to peace" (Colossians 3:15 NIV).

> *Lord, thank You for all the ways You have blessed me. Give me eyes to see Your provision and an attitude that focuses on my blessings and the good things You have given me.*

100

We know that in all
things God works for
the good of those who
love him, who have
been called according
to his purpose.

ROMANS 8:28 NIV

*P*aul's words in Romans 8:28 could easily be referred to as one of the crown jewels of the New Testament. He instructed his readers that regardless of what happens to us in life, God will work every situation for our good. The only condition for this promise is that we love God and are called according to His purpose. With this promise in mind, as believers in Jesus Christ, we can live life with freedom and confidence that even our most painful circumstances will ultimately be used for our good. Even when people inflict harm or tragedy strikes, we can remain confident. In the Old Testament, when Joseph was confronted with his brothers, who had sold him into slavery, he saw how God had worked the situation in his favor and could say, "You intended to harm me, but God intended it for good" (Genesis 50:20 NIV). This promise gives us the confidence to live in the present, with no bitterness about the past or fear of the future.

> *Lord, please take every circumstance in my life and work them all for good. I pray I will live with confidence that even my greatest heartaches will turn out for my good and Your glory.*

Notes

Chapter 1

1. Stuart K. Weber, *Holman New Testament Commentary: Matthew*, ed. Max Anders (Nashville, TN: Broadman & Holman, 2000), 169.

Chapter 25

2. Warren W. Wiersbe, *Be Worshipful: Glorifying God for Who He Is*, Old Testament Commentary: Psalms 1–89 (Colorado Springs: David C. Cook, 2004), 107.

Chapter 26

3. Bert Dominy, "Hope," *Holman Bible Dictionary*, ed. Trent C. Butler (Nashville, TN: Broadman & Holman, 1991), 665.

Chapter 27

4. Wiersbe, 171.

Chapter 31

5. Wiersbe, 165.

Chapter 35

6. D. A. Carson, *Basics for Believers: An Exposition of Philippians* (Grand Rapids, MI: Baker Academic, 1996), 119–20.

Chapter 45

7. *ESV Study Bible* (Wheaton, IL: Crossway, 2008), 2211.

Chapter 48

8. John MacArthur, *The MacArthur New Testament Commentary: Romans 1–8* (Chicago, IL: Moody, 1991), 437.

Chapter 56

9. Wiersbe, *Old Testament Commentary*, 171–73.

Chapter 58

10. Wiersbe, 73.

Chapter 65

11. *ESV Study Bible*, 2053.

Chapter 78

12. John MacArthur, *The MacArthur New Testament Commentary: 1 & 2 Thessalonians* (Chicago, IL: Moody, 2002), 313.

Chapter 90

13. John MacArthur, *The MacArthur New Testament Commentary: John 1–11* (Chicago, IL: Moody, 2006), 306.

Chapter 92

14. D. Martyn Lloyd-Jones, *Studies in the Sermon on the Mount* (Grand Rapids, MI: Eerdmans, 1960), 40–41.

Chapter 94

15. Carson, *Basics for Believers*, 112.

Chapter 97

16. *ESV Study Bible*, 1487.